Learn Reading Skills

Colour each picture as you finish each page.

Written by Jillian Harker and Geraldine Taylor
Illustrated by Bobbie Spargo

Alphabet party: sounds and letters

Who is going to the party? Point to each person in turn and say who they are. What **sound** does each begin with? Can you find the letter which makes that sound?

astronaut bear cat dinosaur elephant
fairy ghost horse insect juggler king lion

magician nurse octopus pirate queen robot sailor
tortoise umbrella vet wolf X-ray yacht zebra

Parent point: The sound-letter link is the first step to actual reading. When your child understands this, progress to pointing to a letter of the alphabet and asking for the sound and the fancy-dress character that begins with that sound.

First sounds

Circle the things that begin with the sound t.

Circle the things that begin with the sound **b**.

What sound does your name begin with?
What sounds do your friends' names begin with?

Parent point: At this stage of early reading the initial sound provides a vital phonic clue to the word. Play 'I spy' using the sounds of letters. Say sounds gently and express the sound as purely as possible. For example, 't' should be pronounced 't' and not 'tuh', 'm' as 'mmm' not 'muh', and so on.

Last sounds

What sound does **bed** end with? Say the words below.

bed

hat t

foot t ✗

shop p

mop p

dad d ✓

head d ✓

ship p

hood d ✓

wood d ✓

meat t

shed d ✓

bread d ✓

boot t

lid d ✓

Tick the words which end with the same sound as bed.
Which letter makes this sound?

Rhyme time

Draw lines to link the words that rhyme.

Can you read and remember this rhyme?

Scat the rat dances on a hat
Stig the pig does a jig in a wig
Pog the dog takes a jog in the fog
Tug the bug runs around a jug
Sly the fly zooms about in the sky
Glee the bee buzzes under the tree

Parent point: A knowledge of rhyme helps awareness of sound patterns as a preparation for phonic work and reinforces the link between sounds and letters. Memory work is vital for reading. Help your child to read and remember this rhyme. Use picture clues to help, too. Can your family make up names and rhymes for other animals? Try: cat, goat, snake, fox, etc.

Clap the beats

Clap the beats as you say each **animal**. How many beats does each one have? Which animal has the most beats? Now clap the beats as you say the animals' **names**. Which name has the most beats?

Parent point: Knowing that words can be broken down into syllables helps a child to deal with unfamiliar words in reading. In this exercise, beats are syllables. Clap the beats of children's names, favourite foods, toys, etc to show that words can be broken down into parts.

Fun 'doing' words

Look at the pictures and read the words.
Draw a star by things you like doing.

sleeping

hiding

digging

sharing

running

hugging

Parent point: Pictures are vital context clues to reading. Point to the word and read it with your child. Write the words on small pieces of card and encourage your child to match them to the word and picture. Make a list of the verbs (doing words) your child can do and add to it gradually. Encourage your child to illustrate the list.

Out and about: signs

How many of the words in the picture can you read?
Tick the boxes.

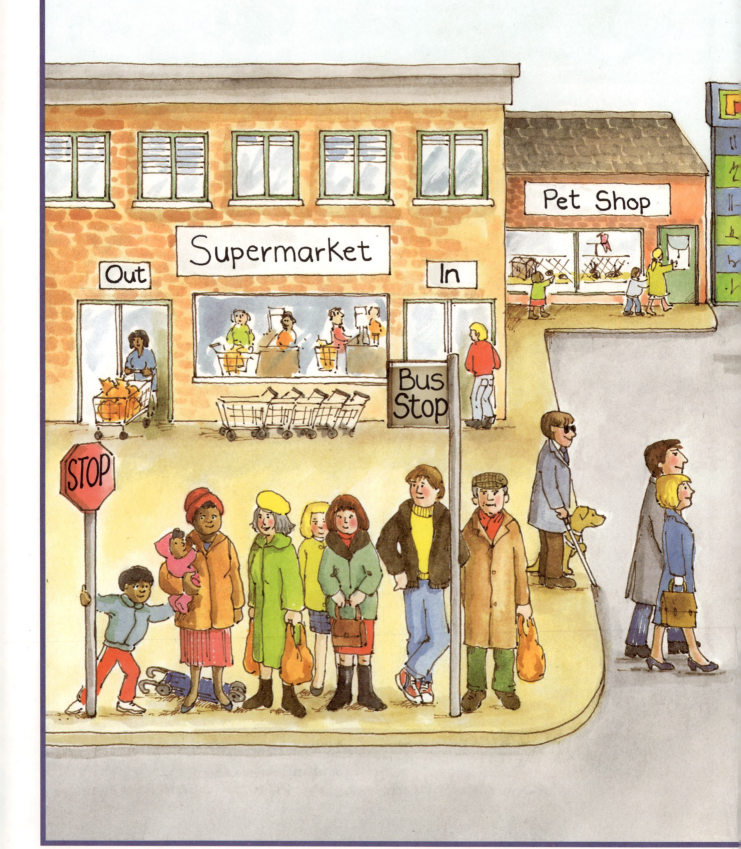

Supermarket ✓

Pet Shop ✓

Garage ✓

In ✓

Out ✓

Car Wash ✓

Cinema ✓

Telephone ✓

Entrance ✓

Bus Stop ✓

STOP

Parent point: Noticing signs and words in the world around us is very important for early reading. Encourage your child to look for and read these wherever you go.

Wet walk

Make up actions to go with the poem.

Let's go on a wet walk
Let's go on a wet walk

Catch the raindrops in your hand
Catch the raindrops as they land

Let's go on a wet walk
Tiny puddles, see them grow
Here's a big one, in we go

Let's go on a wet walk
Blue and yellow, red and green
The biggest rainbow
We've ever seen

We went on a wet walk

Can you remember this poem? Can you read it?

Parent point: Memory plays a vital part in reading. Read this rhyme together and see when your child has the confidence to say it alone. Why not go on a wet walk and say this rhyme?

Underline the words you can read.

shell   chunk   white   choose

cheese   sheet   shirt

chocolate   shore   whiskers

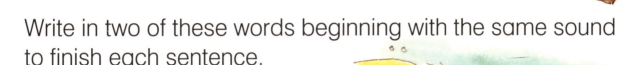

Write in two of these words beginning with the same sound to finish each sentence.

Look at the _shell_ on the _shore_.

The wind blew the _sheet_ and the _shirt_ on the washing line.

Cut me a _chunk_ of _cheese_, please.

Would you like to _choose_ a _chocolate_?

The cat has long, _white whiskers_.

Parent point: Children need to understand that sometimes letters combine to make a special sound, for example, sh, ch, wh. What other words can your child think of that begin with these sounds?

Tongue twisters: letter blends

Can you read these?

flapping flag swooping swallow blue blouse

green grass slimy slug sticky stamp

floating fly swimming swan grey grub

slippery slide black blot steep stairs

Draw a line to join the pairs of pictures that begin with the same sounds.

Read these tongue twisters as fast as you can.

A **bl**ack **bl**ot on a **bl**ue **bl**ouse.

A **gr**ey **gr**ub in the **gr**een **gr**ass.

A **sl**imy **sl**ug on a **sl**ippery **sl**ide.

A **st**icky **st**amp on **st**eep **st**airs.

A **sw**ooping **sw**allow with a **sw**imming **sw**an.

A **fl**oating **fl**y with a **fl**apping **fl**ag.

Parent point: Alliteration (words following or near each other and beginning with the same sound) and tongue twisters are good ways of reinforcing sound and letter patterns. Make up your own family tongue twisters. Play a game: Say the noun, eg grass. Can your child remember which word described it? Say the adjective, eg sticky. Can your child remember which word it described?

Who's who? Two letters, one sound

Who is speaking? Link each animal with the correct speech bubble.

Sound search

The words in each list have the same sound in them. Can you read the list and ring the sound in each word.

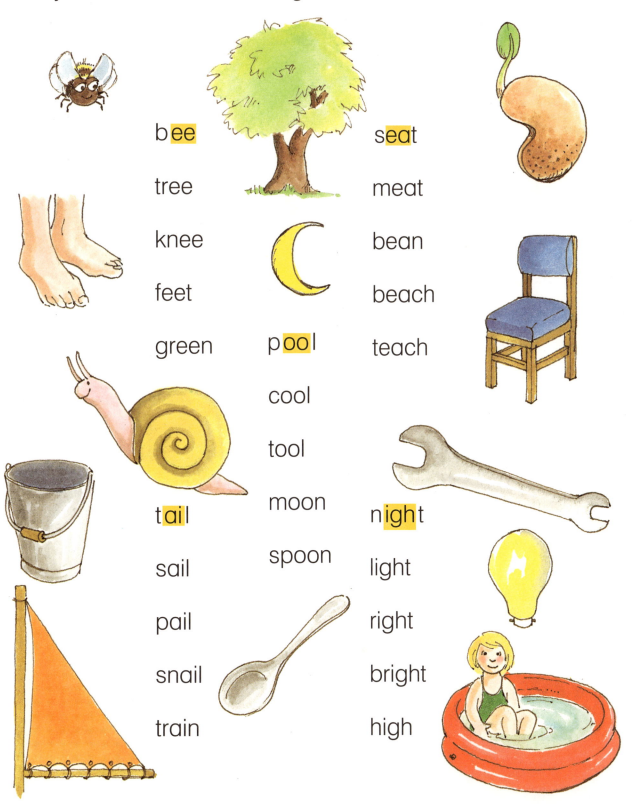

b**ee**   s**ea**t
tree   meat
knee   bean
feet   beach
green   p**oo**l   teach
        cool
        tool
t**ai**l   moon   n**igh**t
sail   spoon   light
pail   right
snail   bright
train   high

Parent point: Children need to understand that sometimes letters combine to make a special sound. Help your child to read these lists. Can you think of other words to add?

No place for a bee

Zig-zag the bee was lost once again. He buzzed loudly round and round in circles and wondered which way to go. While Zig-zag was busy in a purple flower, his friends had gone home without him.

Zig-zag spotted a slimy slug sliding slowly along the path.
"Can I come home with you?" asked Zig-zag.
"You know I live in the long, green grass," said the slug.
"It's no place for a bee. You can't come home with me."

Zig-zag flew over a pond. He spotted a frog splashing in the water.
"Can I come home with you?" asked Zig-zag.
"You know I live deep down in a cool pool," said the frog. "It's no place for a bee. You can't come home with me."

Zig-zag zoomed past a tree. He spotted a blackbird chasing a grey grub.
"Can I come home with you?" asked Zig-zag.
"You know I live with my chicks in a secret nest," said the blackbird. "It's no place for a bee. You can't come home with me."

Zig-zag buzzed into a wood. He spotted a fox digging a hole.

"Can I come home with you?" asked Zig-zag.

"You know I live in a dark den," said the fox.

"It's no place for a bee. You can't come home with me."

"No one wants me."

Zig-zag flew into a garden. He spotted a girl watering the flowers.

"Can I come home with you?" asked Zig-zag.

"Oh, Zig-zag," said the girl. "My house is no place for a bee. You know your home's in the hive under the tree. That's the best place for a bee."

Buzzzz.

Parent point: Children's reading progresses when words learned previously are reinforced and interesting new words are introduced. Read this story with your child and talk about the different ways each character would speak.

How, when and where? (Adverbs)

Tick all the words which show how **you** like to do each of these things.

I like to talk
- sadly ☐
- loudly ☐
- sometimes ☐
- happily ✓

I like to run
- backwards ☐
- uphill ☐
- downhill ☐
- fast ✓

I like to jump
- high ✓
- sideways ☐
- quickly ☐
- noisily ☐

I like to read alone ✓
daily ☐
nightly ☐
quietly ☐

I like to paint well ☐
messily ☐
beautifully ✓
weekly ☐

I like to sing softly ✓
loudly ☐
badly ☐
happily ☐

Parent point: Adverbs are words which describe how, when or where we do things. Awareness of the variety of these develops a child's interest in reading. Play the activity game. Name an activity, (eg skipping) and see how many different ways your child can think of doing it.

Frog facts

Read these pages. Ask a grown-up to help if you like.

1 Frogs lay their eggs in jelly. Look for frogspawn early in the year.

2 The eggs change shape and turn into tadpoles. The tail comes first. The back legs grow slowly.

3 After a while, the front legs grow and the tail begins to shrink. The little frogs crawl out of the water.

4 The frogs hop away to find a damp place to live. They eat spiders and worms.

5 As the weather gets colder, frogs hibernate. Some dig a hole at the bottom of a pond. Others stay in a hole on land.

6 Frogs sleep all through the winter. Next year they will mate and lay more eggs.

Can you answer these questions? Circle the correct picture.

Where do frogs lay their eggs?

Which comes first?

What do frogs eat?

Where do frogs hibernate?

Parent point: Learning interesting facts encourages children's reading. Read this together and help your child to find out about other animals.

Find out fast

If you wanted to find out about these things, which book would you look in?

dinosaurs

jellyfish

koala bears

zebras

helicopters

X-rays

submarines

elephants

icebergs

windmills

computers

Parent point: Dictionary skills are very important in helping children to develop their understanding of words. Match things at home with the alphabet books on this page to give additional practice.